SPOTLIGHT ON
CIVIC COURAGE
HEROES OF CONSCIENCE™

THE 14TH DALAI LAMA

SPIRITUAL LEADER OF TIBET

Jeanne Nagle

Rosen YA

New York

Published in 2018 by The Rosen Publishing Group, Inc.
29 East 21st Street, New York, NY 10010

Library of Congress Cataloging-in-Publication Data

Names: Nagle, Jeanne, author.
Title: The 14th Dalai Lama : spiritual leader of Tibet / Jeanne Nagle.
Description: New York : Rosen Publishing, 2018. | Series: Spotlight on civic courage: Heroes of conscience | Audience: Grades 5–10. | Includes bibliographical references and index.
Identifiers: LCCN 2017011619| ISBN 9781538380819 (library bound) | ISBN 9781538380796 (pbk.) | ISBN 9781508177456 (6 pack)
Subjects: LCSH: Bstan-ʹdzin-rgya-mtsho, Dalai Lama XIV, 1935-–Juvenile literature. | Dalai lamas—Biography—Juvenile literature. | Tibet Autonomous Region (China)—History—Juvenile literature.
Classification: LCC BQ7935.B777 N34 2017 | DDC 294.3/923092 [B] —dc23
LC record available at https://lccn.loc.gov/2017011619

Manufactured in the United States of America

On the cover: After Chinese troops invaded Tibet (background), the fourteenth Dalai Lama, Tenzin Gyatso (foreground), faced exile and a loss of power. Through it all, he has led his people toward the promise of a free Tibet.

CONTENTS

THE SITUATION IN TIBET

T ibet is nestled high in the foot-hills of the Himalayas, a mountain range in Asia. It borders several countries, most notably India to the south and, to the north, China.

Once a powerful kingdom in its own right, Tibet is now the subject of tension and disputes. The Chinese government has made Tibet an autonomous region, meaning it is part of China but with limited freedoms. Tibetans, however, insist that their country should be a totally free and independent state, as it was before China seized political control in the 1950s.

If not for China's desire to regain control over the region, a large portion of the world's populace might never have known that a remote, isolated

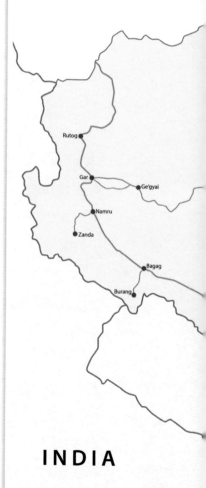

Xinjiang Uy

Rutog

Gar

Ge'gyai

Namru

Zanda

Bagag

Burang

INDIA

place called Tibet even existed. The plight of Tibet and its people—and their fight to become independent once more—might have faded away and been forgotten. But thanks to one leader, the Dalai Lama, it was not.

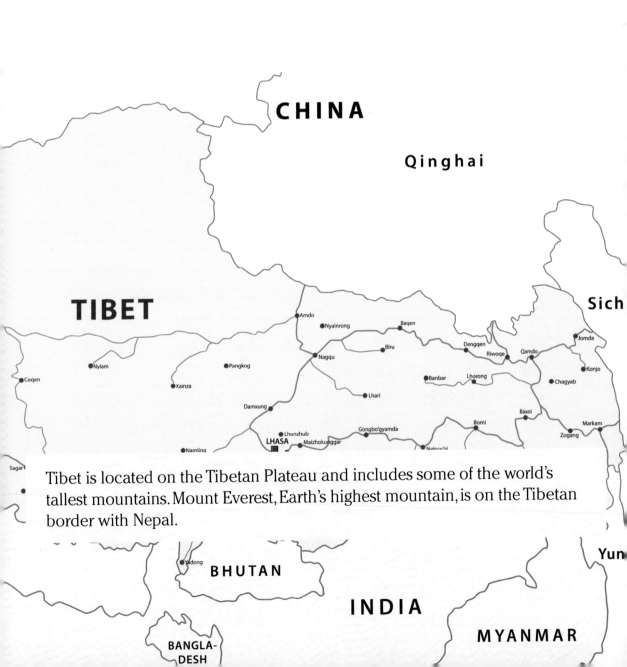

Tibet is located on the Tibetan Plateau and includes some of the world's tallest mountains. Mount Everest, Earth's highest mountain, is on the Tibetan border with Nepal.

Long Live the Dalai Lama

The title given to the religious and political leader of Tibet is Dalai Lama. *Dalai* is the Mongolian word for "ocean," and *lama* is Tibetan for "teacher" or "guru." Many people take this to mean that the Dalai Lama possesses an "ocean of wisdom."

The political element of this position is important, but the spiritual connection goes back farther in history. For centuries, the Dalai Lama has been the head of the main branch of Tibetan Buddhism. It is known as the Yellow Hat sect, or religious order. His followers also believe that he is the god of compassion in human form.

In addition to being a god on Earth, the Dalai Lama is thought to be a very old soul. Buddhists believe in reincarnation, which is when a person's soul comes back to Earth in a different body or form. Starting from the late fourteenth century, there have been fourteen incarnations, or versions, of the Dalai Lama.

This is a statue of the Amitabha Buddha. Those who practice Tibetan Buddhism recite mantras, or sacred phrases, to the Amitabha, known as the Buddha of infinite light.

AND A CHILD SHALL LEAD THEM

The story of the fourteenth Dalai Lama began on July 6, 1935, with the birth of Lhamo Thondup. He was born in the village of Taktser, which is located in the northeastern part of Tibet. His parents, who were farmers, had six other children as well.

Led by a number of signs, a group of Buddhist monks came to the family's farm in the village of Amdo, looking for the reincarnated Dalai Lama. Their attention turned to two-year-old Lhamo Thondup. The child was given a number of tests, which he passed. The monks were convinced that he was the reincarnation of the Dalai Lama.

From there, the monks took Lhamo Thondup first to a nearby monastery, then to the Tibetan capital, Lhasa, for training as a Buddhist monk. In 1940, he was given the holy name Tenzin Gyatso. He was only five years old.

This photograph shows Tenzin Gyatso as he appeared in 1940, when he first began his training as a Buddhist monk.

The fourteenth Dalai Lama is shown here posing for an official portrait in 1950. Tenzin Gyatso was placed in power earlier than planned when the political situation in Tibet grew troubled.

Tenzin Gyatso continued to receive Buddhist philosophy lessons for several years, in preparation for becoming a monk. He was set to assume political leadership of Tibet once he reached the age of twenty, but that timeline was moved up when Chinese troops invaded the country in 1950.

Tenzin was quickly made the head of his country's government in an attempt to keep as much power as possible in Tibetan hands. Even though he was not yet a monk, he was proclaimed the fourteenth Dalai Lama. He was only fifteen, so a regent was given power to rule temporarily until he was old enough to govern on his own.

The Dalai Lama asked the United Nations for help with China, but nothing much was done. Left unchecked, China wrote, and made Tibet sign, the Seventeen-Point Agreement. This document, which gave Tibet some control over its own government, made the country part of China.

FLEEING THE COUNTRY

Once China had control over Tibet, the Dalai Lama was little more than a political figurehead. Yet he stayed in Tibet for years, trying to protect the rights of the Tibetan people. Toward that end, he met with Chinese leaders, including Communist Party leader Mao Zedong, in 1954.

In 1959, the Dalai Lama received an invitation to Beijing that many thought was actually a kidnapping attempt. On March 10, Tibetans showed their anger by surrounding his palace so that he could not leave. This was the beginning of a rebellion known as the Tibetan Uprising.

Fearing for his safety, the Dalai Lama decided he should leave Tibet. Late one night, he snuck out of the palace and headed for Tibet's border with India. He was disguised as one of the Tibetan soldiers who accompanied him. Family members and a handful of teachers joined him on the journey.

The Dalai Lama (*third from right, on a white pony*) fled Tibet with a small group of followers by crossing the Himalayas into India.

A NEW HOME

O n March 13, 1959, the Dalai Lama and his entourage arrived in India, where they were given refuge. In Tibet, the former government was dissolved, and Tibet was declared an autonomous region of China. The Dalai Lama was replaced with a lesser lama who was in favor of Chinese rule.

Once safely settled in India, the Dalai Lama created a government in exile, based in Dharamsala. Because the Chinese had control in Tibet, and the Dalai Lama had no political power in India, it was mostly a government in name only. Soon, however, tens of thousands of loyal followers left Tibet to live in settlements created especially for them by the Indian government. Tenzin Gyatso became the leader of a Tibetan community in exile.

Even though he was living in exile, the Dalai Lama sought to keep Tibetan culture alive, for his followers in India and those back home.

The Dalai Lama smiling as he finally arrives at Birla House in India after leaving Tibet in 1959. Indian independence leader Mahatma Gandhi also had spent time at Birla House.

MAN ON A MISSION

Early in his exile, the Dalai Lama held a press conference in which he publicly rejected the Seventeen-Point Agreement. On March 30, 1959, he made it clear that he had signed the agreement only "in order to save my people and country from the danger of total destruction." He then criticized the Chinese for disregarding the agreement and further suppressing Tibetan freedoms.

This was just the first of many speeches he would make in defense of his homeland. The Dalai Lama became a man on a mission. Every time he spoke or acted, he wanted to make sure that the world knew about Tibet's desire for—and what he believed was the country's right to—freedom and independence.

He knew this would be an uphill battle, though. On March 10, 1960, the anniversary of the Tibetan Uprising, he cautioned that the fight to regain independence for Tibet could take a long time.

Tibetan monks are shown here surrendering to Chinese military forces in April 1959, a month after an uprising against China began. March 10 is still celebrated by Tibetans who oppose Chinese rule.

STEPS TOWARD DEMOCRACY

Through the years, the Dalai Lama did more than give lip service to the idea of a free and independent Tibet. In addition to holding press conferences and giving speeches, he put his intentions down on paper.

In 1963, he wrote a constitution for Tibet that could be used by a freely elected government within the country. The document outlined principles for how the country should be run, blending democratic concepts of social and economic justice with Buddhist doctrines of peace and enlightenment.

In a foreword to the constitution, the Dalai Lama stated that he wrote the document "to give the people of Tibet a new hope" that they would one day live in a free and democratic society. But, as it turns out, the constitution was not merely wishful thinking. The exiled Tibetan government in Dharamsala used the constitution as a guideline.

The Dalai Lama speaking to the press shortly after fleeing Tibet for India. Press conferences have been one way the Dalai Lama has found to express his thoughts and beliefs.

LIFE ON THE ROAD

Traditionally, Dalai Lamas had ruled mainly out of their palaces, not venturing far from home. Out of necessity, however, the fourteenth Dalai Lama became much more of a globetrotter. He has traveled around the world, far away from his home base in Dharamsala, to promote peace and speak about the Tibetans' desire for political independence.

His first trip abroad occurred in 1967, when he visited Japan and Thailand. Throughout the 1970s, he traveled throughout Europe, as well as to the United States and Canada. During these trips, he met with heads of state and the leaders of the world's religions. He also was invited to speak at colleges and universities, which enabled him to share his messages with a wider audience.

The Dalai Lama had an agenda in mind when he took these trips. His talks, both private and public, focused on two topics: sharing and explaining the Buddhist faith and keeping Tibet in the public eye.

Tenzin Gyatso is shown here during a meeting with the archbishop of Canterbury, Michael Ramsey, during a trip to England in 1973.

A Five-Point Peace Plan

In 1979, the Dalai Lama reached out to Chinese government officials for the first time since leaving Tibet. His older brother, Gyalo Thondup, met with Deng Xiaoping, the Communist Party leader at the time, to see what could be done about normalizing relations between China and Tibet. Deng held firm that Tibet must remain a part of China. This was the first of several attempted negotiations with China by the Tibetan government in exile.

In 1987, the Dalai Lama returned to the United States to address Congress, hoping to win support for his Five-Point Peace Plan. Rather than being an olive branch, wherein Tibet tried to appease China in order to bring an end to hostilities, the plan was a statement of Tibet's expectations for achieving lasting peace in the region. Chief among these points was China pulling settlers and military forces out of Tibet and agreeing to stay out of Tibetan affairs.

Tenzin Gyatso's older brother Gyalo Thondup
served as a representative of the Dalai Lama in
negotiations with China in the 1970s.

PROPOSING A COMPROMISE

China, of course, soundly rejected the Five-Point Peace Plan. Because the Chinese government was in a position of power, it didn't feel the need to give in to what they saw as the Dalai Lama's demands.

Disappointed but determined, the Dalai Lama decided to try another approach. A year after addressing the US Congress, he spoke before the general assembly of the European Parliament, which was the governing body of the European Union. This time, rather than taking a hard line on Tibetan independence, he proposed a plan in which Tibet would run its own government but work with China regarding national and foreign matters. Because it was proposed

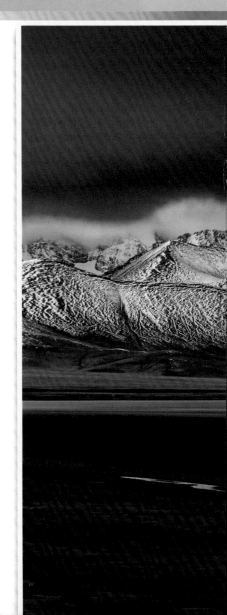

in Strasbourg, France, the plan became known as the Strasbourg Proposal.

This compromise plan drew from the Dalai Lama's Buddhist faith. Buddhism teaches that believers should take a "middle way" approach to life, which emphasizes balance and acceptance of multiple viewpoints.

The sun rises over Lake Nam, a holy site in Tibet. Regaining access to such sacred spaces may have motivated the Dalai Lama's attempts to negotiate with China over Tibetan rule.

HONORED FOR HIS EFFORTS

As many might have expected, the Chinese government flatly rejected the plan put forth in Strasbourg. The proposal was well received throughout the European Union and in the United States, however, and earned the Dalai Lama a lot of respect within the international community. Another party that was impressed by his ongoing efforts was the Norwegian Nobel Committee, which awarded him the Nobel Peace Prize in 1989. The organization noted that the Dalai Lama was given the honor, in part, because "he had showed willingness to compromise and seek reconciliation despite brutal violations" by China against the Tibetan people.

Instead of using the money that came with the award for his own enrichment—which would have been against his principles as a Buddhist monk—the Dalai Lama established the Foundation for Universal Responsibility. The foundation runs programs that encourage and celebrate diversity, teach ethics, and support peaceful coexistence.

His Holiness the Dalai Lama is shown here receiving the Nobel Peace Prize in Oslo, Norway. Presenting him with the award is Nobel Committee member Egil Aarvik.

Another example of the Dalai Lama practicing what he preaches came in 2012, when he won the Templeton Prize. This award honors those who exhibit spirituality in action, through "insight, discovery, or practical works." The Dalai Lama was chosen because he taught that ethics and the Buddhist principles of nonviolence and harmony were universal and worth defending.

Tenzin Gyatso is photographed while addressing the audience in attendance when he was given the 2012 Templeton Prize.

The majority of the approximately $1.8 million in prize money attached to the award was given to the charity Save the Children, to be used in his adopted homeland, India. The organization focuses on children's rights and also provides aid to families during times of crisis.

A smaller portion of the prize money was reserved for education through an organization cofounded by the Dalai Lama called the Mind and Life Institute. It brings together the seemingly unconnected worlds of science and faith so that contemplative practices, such as meditation, might lead to deeper and more far-reaching scientific discoveries.

REFORMS FOR THE HERE AND NOW

Since 1963, the Tibetan government in exile had been operating, more or less, under the constitution that had been created for a future independent Tibet. Within this structure, the Dalai Lama appointed ministers to the Assembly of Tibetan People's Deputies (ATPD)—the equivalent of a parliament.

The Tibetan Charter, approved by the Dalai Lama in 1991, changed certain aspects of the way the government in exile was run. Under the charter, more members were added to the ATPD, and they did not need to be approved by the Dalai Lama. The establishment of a judiciary branch also resulted from the charter.

As with the government's original constitution, the charter was designed to blend the traditions and beliefs of the Tibetan people with the basic principles of democracy. It was drafted incorporating the spirit of equality and nondiscrimination found in the United Nations Universal Declaration of Human Rights.

In 1991, the Dalai Lama attended a celebration of the United Nations' International Day of Peace in Dordogne, France.

ANOTHER TIBETAN UPRISING

On March 10, 2008, a group of monks in Tibet marked Tibetan Uprising Day, which commemorates the anniversary of the 1959 uprising, by marching through the streets of Lhasa. One reason for the march was that the monks were trying to secure the release of Tibetans arrested days before. They were being punished for celebrating the Dalai Lama being awarded the US Congressional Gold Medal. In truth, they were also marching to protest years of poor treatment by the Chinese.

After several of the protesters were arrested, the situation took a turn for the worse. Days later, a protest in Lhasa turned violent. Tibetans damaged Chinese businesses, set fires, threw stones at police, and attacked Chinese residents of the city. The Chinese government said that about twenty people died, mostly Chinese.

Carrying a photo of the Dalai Lama, exiled Tibetan monks march in Dharamsala to mark Tibetan Uprising Day in 2008. Protests in Tibet that day turned violent.

The Dalai Lama spoke out against the violence in Lhasa that resulted from the 2008 uprising in that city on March 10.

In the days following the initial violence in and around Lhasa, the uprising spread throughout Tibet and across the border with China. Additionally, Chinese embassies in India (New Delhi) and Nepal were reportedly under attack. More peaceful demonstrations took place in several European and US cities, including New York (outside the United Nations building) and Washington, DC. Tibetan authorities in Dharamsala reported that, all told, more than two hundred Tibetans had died or disappeared following weeks of rioting.

The Chinese government tied the uprising back to Dharamsala when it blamed forces loyal to the Dalai Lama for causing the riots. For his part, the Dalai Lama criticized those who had rioted. As a Buddhist monk, the Dalai Lama was against all forms of violence. As the leader of a country trying to win back its independence, he knew that a confrontation of any kind with China would not achieve that goal. According to some sources, he threatened to resign from his post as Tibetan political leader if the violence did not stop immediately.

CHINESE CRACKDOWN

Since 1959, the Chinese had failed to remove the exiled Dalai Lama, and the things he stood for, from the hearts and minds of his people. However, this was not from lack of trying. Even before the 2008 uprising—and certainly afterward—the Chinese had tried to either minimize or totally erase the influence of the Dalai Lama in Tibet.

They made listening to or reading his speeches a criminal offense. Tibetans were not even allowed to own or display images of their spiritual leader. In 2013, Chinese officials placed stricter restrictions on internet use and ownership of illegal satellite dishes in an attempt to keep news of the Dalai Lama out of Tibetan households.

The Chinese took these steps because they viewed the Dalai Lama as an enemy of the state. They claimed that he was trying to cause a split in a unified China, which included the Tibetan Autonomous Region.

Tenzin Gyatso is shown here greeting the crowd during a speech at the Beacon Theatre in New York City in 2013. That year, China cracked down further on shows of loyalty to the Dalai Lama in Tibet.

CHANGING ROLES

Changes were afoot in Dharamsala in 2011. Feeling that the more democratic way to run the government in exile was to have an elected, secular leader, the Dalai Lama announced that he would resign his position as political head of state. On May 29, 2011, the Dalai Lama signed over political power to the newly elected prime minister, Lobsang Sangay. He kept his position as the spiritual leader of Tibet.

The Dalai Lama had another reason for handing over political power. He was aware that a new incarnation would need to be found to take his place when he died. Chinese leaders had vowed that they would be the ones to choose the new

Dalai Lama, not Tibetan monks. Even if China made good on that threat, they would only be choosing a religious leader. Tibet would still have a political leader who would fight for independence.

The Dalai Lama is shown here embracing his political successor, Lobsang Sangay, as the latter is sworn in as the Tibetan government in exile's newly elected prime minister in 2011.

LIFE AND LEGACY

Many things have changed over the course of the fourteenth Dalai Lama's lifetime. He went from being a farmer's son to being proclaimed the reincarnated spirit of Tibet's most revered spiritual leader. Given the power to rule over the Tibetan government at just fifteen years of age, he had that control taken away by an invading force. Decades later, he willingly gave up political control of Tibet, thus changing the role of the Dalai Lama, possibly for a long time to come.

But some things in his life have been constant. Among these are the Dalai Lama's steadfast commitment to Tibet, its people, and its quest for independence, as well as to the Buddhist principles of peace, harmony, and walking the path of enlightenment.

What the future holds for successive incarnations of the Dalai Lama remains to be seen. But the legacy of the fourteenth Dalai Lama, as a hero of conscience, should live on forever.

The Dalai Lama draws large crowds to hear him speak. Sharing his beliefs and vision for a free Tibet has been his lifelong quest.

GLOSSARY

autonomous Being independent and capable of governing oneself.

compassion The ability to understand another's suffering and feeling compelled to help.

confrontation When two opposing forces meet to fight.

contemplative Dedicated to the spiritual, faith, and devotion.

culture The collected beliefs and customs of a group of people.

democratic Based on a form of government in which the people choose leaders by voting.

doctrine A set of principles or beliefs that guide the actions of a person or group of people.

enlightenment A state of being in which there is no want or suffering.

entourage A group of people who support and help someone who is thought of as their leader.

exile The state of being forced to leave one's country or home.

figurehead Someone who is in charge or has power in name only.

incarnation The physical form of a spirit or soul.

monastery A place where monks live and work together.

plight A difficult or unpleasant situation.

populace Common, or everyday, people.

refuge A safe place that offers shelter or protection.

regent A person who rules a kingdom when the king, queen, or other ruler is unable to rule.

reincarnation One who has been born again and lives in a different body.

secular Being of the world, rather than spiritual or religious.

suppressing Stopping by using force or power.

FOR MORE INFORMATION

Buddhist Association of the United States
2020 Route 301
Carmel, NY 10512
(845) 225-1819
Website: http://www.baus.org/en
Established in 1964, the association is a nonprofit dedicated to sharing Buddhist principles and thought through programs, retreats, and publications.

Dalai Lama Center for Peace and Education
PO Box 3662
Station Terminal
Vancouver, British Columbia
V6B 3Y8
Canada
(604) 215-2352
Website: http://dalailamacenter.org
Facebook: @dalailamacenter
Twitter: @dalailamacenter
YouTube: @Dalai Lama Center for Peace and Education
The center offers programs and events geared toward peaceful and compassionate ways in which to educate children. There is an emphasis on the Dalai Lama's belief that education must balance educating the mind with educating the heart.

International Campaign for Tibet
1825 Jefferson Place NW
Washington, DC 20036
(202) 785-1515
Website: https://www.savetibet.org
Facebook: @InternationalCampaignForTibet
Twitter: @SaveTibetOrg
The International Campaign for Tibet promotes human rights and freedom for all Tibetans. The organization also ventures into Chinese-Tibetan relations.

Office of Tibet
1228 17th Street NW
Washington, DC 20036
(212) 213-5010
Website: http://tibetoffice.org
Facebook: @office.of.tibet
Twitter: @officeoftibetdc
The office solicits support from US and Canadian government representatives, provides education programs on Tibet and its government in Dharamsala, and coordinates the Dalai Lama's visits to North America.

WEBSITES

Because of the changing nature of internet links, Rosen Publishing has developed an online list of websites related to the subject of this book. This site is updated regularly. Please use this link to access this list:

http://www.rosenlinks.com/CIVC/Lama

FOR FURTHER READING

Gray, Nick. *Escape from Tibet: A True Story*. Toronto, ON, Canada: Annick Press, 2014.

Hopkins, Jeffrey. *Kindness, Clarity, and Insight: The Fourteenth Dalai Lama His Holiness Tensin Gyatso*. Ithaca, NY: Snow Lion Publications, 2010.

Kimmel, Elizabeth Cody. *Boy on the Lion Throne: The Childhood of the 14th Dalai Lama*. New York, NY: Flash Point (Macmillan), 2009.

Marsico, Katie. *Buddhism*. North Mankato, MN: Cherry Hill Publishing, 2017.

Nagle, Jeanne. *The Dalai Lama: Spiritual Leader of the Tibetan People*. New York, NY: Rosen Publishing Group, 2014.

Saiwai, Tetsu. *The 14th Dalai Lama: A Manga Biography*. New York, NY: Penguin Books, 2010.

Sis, Peter. *Tibet Through the Red Box*. New York, NY: Farrar, Straus and Giroux, 2014.

Sullivan, Ann Marie, and Chen Jiang-Jiang. *Dalai Lama: Spiritual Leader of Tibet*. Broomall, PA: Mason Crest, 2013.

BIBLIOGRAPHY

Ananthraman, Aravinda. *Puffin Lives: The 14th Dalai Lama*. New York, NY: Puffin Books (Penguin USA), 2011.

BBC News. "Q and A: China and the Tibetans." BBC News Online. August 15, 2011. http://www.bbc.com/news/world-asia-pacific-14533879.

Central Tibetan Administration. "Charter of the Tibetans in Exile." June 14, 1991. http://tibet.net/about-cta/constitution.

Foundation for Universal Responsibility of His Holiness the Dalai Lama, The. "Mission." Retrieved February 2017. http://www.furhhdl.org/mission.

Norwegian Nobel Institute. "The 14th Dalai Lama–Facts." Nobelprize.org. Retrieved February 2017. http://www.nobelprize.org/nobel_prizes/peace/laureates/1989/lama-facts.html.

Office of His Holiness the Dalai Lama. "Birth to Exile." His Holiness the 14th Dalai Lama of Tibet. Retrieved February 2017. http://www.dalailama.com/biography/from-birth-to-exile.

Osnos, Evan. "The Next Incarnation." *New Yorker*. Volume 86, Issue 30, October 4, 2010, p. 63.

Praag, Michael Van Walt. "A Historical Overview of Tibet." The Office of Tibet, Washington, D.C. Retrieved February 2017. http://tibetoffice.org/tibet-info/historical-overview.

Praag, Michael Van Walt. "In Spirit, Tibet's Lamas Resemble Iran's Mullahs; New Peace Initiative." *New York Times.* August 27, 1988. http://www.nytimes.com/1988/08/27/opinion/l-in-spirit-tibet-s-lamas-resemble-iran-s-mullahs-new-peace-initiative-278788.html.

INDEX

ABOUT THE AUTHOR

Jeanne Nagle is a writer and editor in upstate New York who greatly admires the fourteenth Dalai Lama. Her interest and research has lead to books covering the life and mission of His Holiness, including *People You Should Know: Top 101 World Leaders* and *The Dalai Lama: Spiritual Leader of the Tibetan People*.

PHOTO CREDITS